The Fear of Loss

The Fear of Loss

Poems of Love and War

Dominic Margiotta

The Pentland Press Limited
Edinburgh • Cambridge • Durham • USA

First published in 1995 by
The Pentland Press Ltd.
1 Hutton Close
South Church
Bishop Auckland
Durham

British Library Cataloguing in Publication Data.
A Catalogue record for this book is available
from the British Library.

ISBN 1 85821 319 3

Typeset by CBS, Felixstowe, Suffolk
Printed and bound by Antony Rowe Ltd., Chippenham

DEDICATION

In subdued light
By the dying candle flickering flame
I wrote these poems for you.
Read them well
They were not written in heaven
But in hell.

They were not born of laughter
But the fruits of darker years
Written in blood
And the waters of many tears.

Contents

THE SENTRY

The sentry looks out from his hole in the wall
When out of the darkness he hears a voice call
But the drums are all broken,
The soldiers are dead,
The field is deserted,
And the enemy has fled.

Once more it arises o'er the field and behind
As the first wave of madness creeps over his mind,
The flags are all torn
The front is so still
And the cannons are silent
On the brow of the hill.

He cries to his friends but his friends cannot hear
As reason gives way to the poundings of fear,
His courage has broken
He knows he's alone
And the voice in his ear
Is only his own.

He flies from his post with the moon in its wane
With his features bereft of both honour and shame,
The bugles are blowing
The charge has begun,
The dead have arisen
To the beat of the drum.

Morning is breaking, the night clouds have gone,
The birds are all singing their first morning song,
A sentry is standing
With no one in sight
An only survivor
Of a skirmish at night.

THE WARRIOR

By his lonely cave like dwelling
With his arms of wrath and pride,
With no fools to bid him welcome
By that lonely mountain side.

Who but children may approach him
No sweeter sound to him so kind
As the curse men lay upon him,
Oh this warrior of all mankind.

Bridges span his soul whose entry
Are through portals made of sand,
Naught but anger may provoke him
Naught but feathers in his hand.

None so lonely as the dragon
Breathing flames from hidden fires
That are but embers and the ashes
Of all the pain that hate inspires.

From the bastion, through the portal,
Gazing on the fields below,
None but children may engage him
With his tales of long ago.

Warring winds to tempests raging
Storm filled clouds the darker sky
Thunder mocks the heavens to anger
Naught but tears may fill his eye.

Who but heaven may awake him
From the dreams that fill his mind?
Who but angels may defend him
Oh this warrior of all mankind?

THE CENOTAPH

They shall be remembered
In whatever land or clime
They shall not be forgotten
Until the end of time.
The Cenotaph where they sleep
Beneath an eternal flame,
There lies the unwithering wreath
And the praise the proud call fame.

None shall rob them of their glory
Nor to their graves deny,
The wreath, the flower, and the poppy
And the flags that o'er them fly.

But there is a widow standing
With the widows of all the world
Who never cared for glory
Nor the flags to them unfurled.

She is crying for her lover
As the world has cried for years
And the only medal she can bring
Is the medal of her tears.

In her eyes there are no heroes
For love requires no fame,
She would bathe his wounds perhaps
With far more love than shame.

The great may come with flowers
And whatever else they gave,
But she who loved him brought a tear
And laid it on his grave.

WAR MADNESS

In an age when the cannon is silent
And the sword to its sheath has retired,
I dwell on the wars that are over
And the shame which that curse has inspired.
I dwell on the pulpits of madness
Where honour and glory are preached,
Where reason is obscured into darkness
And virtue and prudence impeached.
I dwell on the fear and the rashness
The terror, the grief and the shame
The horrors of death, and the sadness
And the heads buried deep into pain.
I think of the poppy and the anthem
And the flame which burns o'er the dead,
Of the paths which lead not to glory
And the widows who lie in their bed.
The poet who dreams on a pillow
To rekindle that flame ere it dies
With a pen as black as the raven
And a tongue as sweet as his lies.
Of the children who cry for their fathers
In whose eyes no mother can see
The hero they dreamt of in childhood
And the foe whom they fought to be free.
But a tear in their eyes is still lingering
Like a tear on a leaf soon to fall,
A distant drum in the desert is beating
And a bugle is sounding recall.
Then fly away all you children who listen

And curse that song ere it began,
Take up your little toys and hurry
And run away as best you can.

ATLANTA

Atlanta is burning
The skies are aflame
The soldiers are dying
In sorrow and shame,
For the south is retreating
With nowhere to go
While Sherman lays waste
To the sweet Shenandoah.

To Richmond!
To Richmond!
The northerner cries,
While the flames of Atlanta
Are burning the skies,
With none to oppose them
They sweep to the sea
With Richmond before them
And Robert E. Lee.

They gather around him
Like wolves on their prey
While the cannons keep roaring
By night and by day,
But the bugles are silent,
The rout is complete,
The wounded are dying
And the dead are asleep.

The vultures come down
From their abode on the tree
To feast on the slaughter
With shrieking and glee,
Their blood is all dry
Exposed to the sun,
And the jackals are feeding
Undisturbed by the gun.

Atlanta is burning
The skies are aflame
The widows are weeping
In sorrow and shame.
Come, oh! my daughters,
With nowhere to go,
And sing by the waters
Of the sweet Shenandoah.

DESPAIR

Cry out to the Gods
Enough!
Enough!
Cry out to the Gods, enough!
Our ships are out
The sea is rough
Cry out to the Gods, enough!

Cry out to the Gods
Be still!
Be still!
Cry out to the Gods, be still!
Our ships are sinking
They have lost their will
Cry out to the Gods, be still!

Cry out to the Gods
Farewell!
Farewell!
Cry out to the Gods, farewell!
They have found a port
In the bowels of hell
Cry out to the Gods, farewell!

THE WARRIOR'S DREAM

The night cloud comes down on the warrior at last
To lie on his pillow with his dreams of the past,
His sabre is sheathed with his shield by his side
While his horse in its pasture is snorting in pride.

He dreams of his children who await him at home
And the tears of his bride who is weeping alone,
The spoils of their labour that to honour must yield
As the point of his sabre and the blood on his shield.

Too long has he wandered from them to his wars
His first love in the morning from those he adores,
But power esteems no one else but the brave
It prepares him a cradle from birth to the grave.

He stirs for a moment as the wild banners stream
To the pomp and the power that flow through his dream,
He dwells on his marches with an emblem unfurled
To the corners of glory that before him are curled.

But his memories have left him overwrought in his rage
To folly and madness with no will to engage,
And the tears from his eyes fall cold on the rust
As red as the shield that lies in the dust.

For love has returned and his efforts are spent
His honour has lessened and his sabre is bent,
He rises but once as the foe come in streams
To scatter his blood o'er the field of his dreams.

TAMARAND

Were there no Angels there
When Tamarand quit the field,
Our swords unblunted on the blade
The cross our only shield?
Were they not there
When Tamarand
Drove our ranks apart
But trumpets to the trembling ear
But no sword to pierce the heart?
So did we yield to the jeering foe,
To their fluttering flags raised high,
To bend our knee to the crescent moon
And to the shame
Which made us cry?
Did we not beg Saint Michael's aid
As Tamarand sheathed his sword
That lead us meekly to our chains
And he to his reward?
What sorrows now
To heaven's blame,
What coin
To God is paid?
No herald to awake us with his song
No glorious last crusade.
The Christian cross lies buried
Where only jackals lurk
And God has led us to our chains
And our widows to the Turk.

THE CURSE

Cursed be the cannon
The spear
And the shell,
The kings
And the princes
Who over us dwell.
Cursed be the folly
The flag
And the rule,
The hero of madness
And the day of the fool.
Cursed be the anthem
The medal
And flame,
Which burns in our absence
Along with our name.
Cursed be the poppies
The pomp
And the flower,
The emblems of glory
And the symbol of power.
Cursed be the grave
Where the hero lies dead
While the princes together
Lie plotting in bed.

FEAR

Cannon blast
From hill top crest
O'er silence
Loud as thunder,
Unsurprised
They stare,
Without wonder.
Parts of bodies strewn,
Autumn fallen leaves unknown,
Above the unhallowed grave unblown.
Fear masked faces
Laugh or cry,
Mirthless laughter pleads
But reaps no reply.
Silence comes
And buried fear,
And fear of what fear may do,
Unless
All those around,
And on the other side,
Are as fearful too.

THE SOMME

The pale eye of night
The black face of fear
And terror who awaits its commander,
A ghostly parade
A lonely estate
And the hero who dreams of surrender.
The demon!
The demon!
Cries a fool from the field
And all eyes turn to their commander.
But the dead are asleep
While the dawn comes awake
And the fires burn down to an ember.
Tally ho!
Tally Ho!
A trumpet is heard,
Tally ho!
Replies its commander,
But over the hedge
The knights are asleep
With the children they cannot remember.
A maiden in white
In the pale eye of night,
Oh come my beloved commander!
But the soldiers have gone
From the fields of the Somme
And the dead lie asleep without number.

THE RETREAT

Sweet Miriam the battles are over
The soldiers in blue have all gone,
But your lover lies dead in the valley
And the bugler's retreat is his song.

It rises o'er the hills and the rivers,
It lies on the mists of the lake,
It dies with the sun in its setting
It is born with the dawn in its wake.

It is heard by the wolf and the eagle
The leopard, the deer, and the crow
It smoulders in the fires of Atlanta
It hangs o'er the Shenandoah.

And your lover too will have heard it
As he fell in that final retreat
With the sweet stars of God above him
And the earth of the south at his feet.

And Sheridan too will have heard it
As he flung his wild oaths with his flags
That arose like a standard of eagles
While the south lay scattered in rags.

THE REPLY

How old are you son?
Asks the veteran soldier.
Fourteen, sir,
Comes the reply.
The veteran soldier turns away
To listen to a whippoorwill cry.

Will they attack, sir?
Asks the young recruit.
Perhaps they may,
Comes the reply.
The young recruit turns away
For fear that he might cry.

Then the bugler sounds at last
Retreat
And the union soldiers fly.

It is over son,
Says the veteran soldier.
From the trench
There is no reply.

THE CHARGE OF THE LIGHT BRIGADE

Loud o'er the field the lancer's cry
Proud points the sparkling blade,
Proud flies their banner to the wind,
Oh the charge of the Light Brigade.

Through the smoke filled holocaust
With death on every side,
Towards the waiting foe they charge
Their emblems full of pride.

Past the Russian heavy cannon
Through the exploding shell,
Towards death's gaping grave
Towards the gates of hell.

Full flight the horse into the pit,
Cruel spouts the cannon's flame,
As if the sky was made of metal
And the earth made of rain.

No thoughts of victory lay behind
The rage that drove them past
The cauldrons of the burning tide
And the fame that held them fast.

But onwards ever onwards,
Towards the final mile,
The unchallenged foe with awe inspired
Bequeaths an awarding smile.

Forward ever forward,
To the bugler's shrill command
Till he falls beneath the thundering hooves
With the bugle in his hand.

Till at last the cannon's merciless flame
Dies out from sheer excess
And o'er the field but silence reigns
And the quieter tones of death.

But one hour of courage to their ruin
While the foe looks down in awe
Crowned in regal robes of shame
And laurel leaves of straw.

Six hundred lancers died that day,
Not a single yard was won,
None but the brave lay dying there
Beneath the Crimean sun.

Loud across a land proclaimed
Their honour to the dust
But failure bears some other name
To God alone its trust.

THE GRAVE

This plot of earth
Is yours,
Of all you see, lieutenant,
You are the captain of the field,
Its landlord
And its tenant.

THE PACIFIST

Not to them the honour or the blame
All men's faults lie buried with their shame,
Men may mock
But the angels alone applaud
And leave their swords unsheathed
By the warm left hand of God.
Cursed by the injuries they would endure
For a cause though just
To them impure,
Seeking amid the ruins
At least apart
The tears of all the world
That broke their heart.
They were the heroes
Who from victory fled
Amid the last remains of the unhonoured dead,
Who still could cry upon their tomb
Remembering them as children
In their mother's womb.

UNREQUITED LOVE

Of sorrows there is none so great
As that which comes to him
Who having loved with all his heart
Has loved alas in vain.

For he who loves but loves alone
No solace can be found,
He dies in silken robes adorned
Mid pleasures all around.

He may turn towards the heavens
From this earthbound withering sod,
But the pleasures he found in loving
He shall not find in God.

The heart once pierced must perish
The wounds too deep to heal,
For a woman's kiss to him denied
With a love she does not feel.

He knows her love is over
He sees the final scene,
He may cling to the silken veil
But as in a vanished dream.

The grief is over burdened,
Too full the flooding well,
He sees the final curtain fall
And he knows it all too well.

MELANCHOLY

If melancholy be to the poet's mind
What love is to the heart
Then why pervert the fatal flight
Of the pale Venetian dart?

For who could bear the Promethean fires
Should he set those flames alight
With the tales he stole from the demon's soul
And the caravans which roll by night?

Must he then betray the muse's spark
And pose in some more gentle clime,
Like Byron in his latter years
Or Shelley in his prime?

Must he appease the plebeian ears
With songs of celestial melody,
Like the lyrics of the troubadour
Or the vagabonds of Italy?

Is he to be condemned who alas is dead
To all else, save that of sin,
To curse the dreadful dreams without
And the dreadful dreams within?

To be damned in hell who never knew
One peaceful hour 'mid graceless gloom,
Whose only joy was the ticking clock
And the tolling bells of doom.

To sadness he must ever cling
To the dirge and sad lament
What grace to him was given
That grace was badly spent.

To him no laughter amid the tears
No concubine to sell
Her love at a price he cannot pay
With a tale he cannot tell.

THE SONG

I heard her sing a song at evening
Beneath one lonely trembling starry sky,
And by her listening tulips gathering
While the river Melfe passed her lapping by.
She sang with so much grace and longing
As though her heart was breaking, and her tears
Fell so lightly on the flowers around her
That song still haunts me and it will for years.
I have not seen her since nor heard her
And I often wonder who she was or why
But still I wait for her each evening
While the river Melfe passes me lapping by.
And so perplexed I ponder and I wonder
Though many a year since then has come and gone
Was I the only one who heard her singing
And did I love the singer or the song?

BETRAYAL

Remorse
And reproach,
The guilt
And the blame,
The sweet touch of softness
The sound of your name,
All these have left me
The heart feels no more
And my visions of trust
No love can restore.

The shame
And the folly,
The contempt
And the scorn,
Your vows all around you
Lie tattered and torn.
The heart may forgive
But cannot forget
The day you betrayed me
I can only regret.

BETRAYED

Often in his eyes I saw your image,
To him the most pure, the most sublime;
And he, who made so much of honour and pride
Flung them both away and honours you by his side.

Now if remorse in me finds no place
Yet for his forgiveness would I repent my sin,
Not for the virtue I took from you
But for the honour I took from him.

THE FAULT

When we were together we spoke
But we did not listen.
We were strangers then
We are strangers now,
Too many things to love
But not each other.
When you left I did not cry
The fault was never really yours
Nor mine.

THE LAKE

The night clouds have gathered
And the stars are awake,
As I stand by my Mary
Where she lies 'neath the lake.
The stillness reminds me
I mourn on my own
While my Mary lies sleeping
In that lake all alone.
No peace in her dwelling
Till I lie by her side
Where warm she once rested
When she lay as my bride.
Now colder than seashells
Amid them in sleep
As cold as the coral
As cold as the deep.

LOVE AND TIME

The heart must bleed
And the heart must break
And our loves with time must perish,
'Tis in dreams alone the vanished scenes
The love our hearts would cherish.
The flow of life's most wayward streams
Are damned up in marsh bound rivers,
And the lily for all its virgin white
Must flow on until it withers.
For the ivy grows upon the wall
And no lilies passing by
Can fill the heart with so much love
As the tears that fill the eye.

LOVERS

In a sitting-room of silence
A lonely couple sit
By a fire of dying embers
Neath a lamp light
Dimly lit.
Before them
And above them
All around their shadows play,
A web of dancing figures
Dressed in dreary garments grey.
The fireplace is a memory
Of flickering flames that dance
About them
Like an open book
Of lovers and romance.
But sullen silence interrupts,
The page around them spreads
A quiet good night of dreams apart
As cold as their separate beds.

THE INSULT

They say that you are fair
With grace in abundance given
Whose charms no doubt
To the perjured eye
Were less of earth than heaven.

But I of grace have never known
Nor with your charms acquainted
Nor with the angelic brush
They say your face had painted.

So let them boast who made you most
Alike the flowers at dawning,
That filled their hearts with such esteem
And no doubt with so much longing.

But I have your portrait in my room
Which a friend to me has given
And I swear by Jove
And all else above
You are more of earth
Than heaven.

LOVE

Oh dearer to me than life
When all life I found in you
To take from it
Its every dream
And make those dreams come true

And yet how many times I saw
Your tears from hidden springs
And while you cried,
You smiled the more,
Like the song the thornbird sings.

For much of sorrow have you known
Which you forbade me see
Ah, so well hidden those silent tears,
And so unknown to me.

Yet shall I take them now
And cherish them as gold
Both for the love within your heart
And the tales you never told.

For love, as tears, though dearly bought,
Is the dearer when life is gone
To make of pain love's greatest gift
Like the thornbird's sweetest song.

THE MARRIAGE

The priest
And the altar,
The bread
And the wine,
A ring on her finger
And a promise divine.
But the marriage was over
Before it began
The bells are still ringing
But the guests have all gone.

FLORA

Do not speak to me of Flora,
Unless you speak of shame,
I despise her memory
And I despise her name.
Let no harsher words than these
Upon her tomb stone rest,
Better by far the earth around her
And the worm upon her breast.

DEAD CHILD

Softly to his parents crying,
Mother and father come and see,
Teardrops on my brothers' faces
Tears you never shed for me.

Tolls the bell upon a steeple tolling,
Mother and father come and see,
All the flowers around me growing
All the flowers denied to me.

Wearily the parents waken,
Oh mother and father why do you sleep?
Can't you see the rain is falling
Like the tear drops on my cheek?

Loud blows the wind of mourning,
Oh mother and father hear it slip
Through the covers of my bedside
With cold wet kisses upon my lips.

A LAST ROSE

Last of the summer roses
Both white and red
That I have gathered around your bed.
Oh let me hurry before the snow
Hides the garden
From where they grow,
And in the ice cold winter gloom
No more roses around your room.
Oh where shall I find
A rose to bring
To make you happy
Until the spring?

IN REMEMBRANCE

I shall remember you
I shall not forget,
Nor shall I seek comfort
Nor aught else
That may distract me of your memory.
At the altar of your grave
I shall give to life
What it has taken,
Nor shall I regret the tears
Save those which I have caused you
Which I shall repay with tears
That have no end,
From eyes that see no more
The joys
And the sweetness of this life.
All I see is a face
I shall never see again
All I know is night
From the break of day.

THE PAST

Oh sweet
Sweet opiate,
Yesterday's dreams,
The refuge and balm
Of all our years.
To conjure phantoms
Of our past delights
And chill the memory
Of a thousand tears.

LAURA

Laura, the sun sets upon your grave,
Blood red on the roses play,
And all around their perfumes mild
Rest upon you Laura,
And my child.

O could I be with you forever
And never leave your side,
O most beloved, to whom I gave
My child a cradle
And to you the grave.

THE DREAM

Within the palace of her dream
Beneath the chandeliers
Come the golden knights in armour
And the gallant cavaliers.
And lovers too from far and wide
And youths who to her pride
Come to kiss her full red lips
And languish by her side.
But the dream is merely fancy
And alas does fade away
Into the purple breaking dawn
Of the vulgar common day.
She looks around her bedroom
And the trinkets of her pride,
She cries
And she cries
And she cries alone
With the old man by her side.

THE LAKE

Ah that lake!
That lake!
That dismal lake!
That lake where you lie asleep,
Within its waters cold and grey
Oh so dark and deep!
Mournful trees around you gather
The willow
And the pine,
A sorrowful song the lark does sing
But not as sad as mine.
Ah that lake!
That lake!
That dismal lake!
That lake where you lie asleep,
You have left me no other place to mourn
Save by the dismal lake.

FLORA MACDONALD'S LAMENT

Oh can it be,
Oh can it be,
I'll no see him again!
Frae morn
Tae night
I'll wait in vain
But he'll no come back again.
Oh can it be,
Oh can it be,
When I awake
He'll no be there,
With the sunlight in his bonnie eyes
And the heather in his hair.
Oh can it be,
Oh can it be,
He'll no lay on my breast
When frae the wars he came to me
Within my arms to rest.
Oh can it be,
Oh can it be,
He'll no come back again,
Oh Bonnie Cherlie,
My bonnie prince,
I'll wait for ye in vain.
Nae mair the piprock's sad lament
Shall bid ye welcome hame,
Nor anxious bairns smile wae glee
Tae hear yer bonnie name.
Sunk in winter's lowly bed

I cry
But I cry in vain,
For bonnie Cherlie,
My bonnie prince,
Will no come back again.

DALMENY

When the mist over Melfe is falling
And the dew lies cold on the rose
I remember Dalmeny and the Almond
And my thoughts to that river now flows.

I remember the woods where we gathered
The young branch that fell from the tree,
The dandelion leaves and the cherries
And the flowers that grew by the sea.

We walked across the shores of Dalmeny
To the sound of the waves by our side
That fell on the sands with a murmur
O'er the crest of the fast flowing tide.

We spoke of the land of our childhood
Where the olive and the citrus fruit grow
And the sun which commanded the heavens
And the mountains were covered in snow.

The church in a circle of sunlight,
Our wedding and the love we maintained,
Through the years in spite of our exile
And the joys in our hearts we retained.

But those joys have all vanished, and Dalmeny
Remains in my thoughts like a dream,
And when I weep my tears are now falling
On the waters of that sweet flowing stream.

THE FRIEND

Oh my friend,
My friend,
It is near the end,
We have drifted too far apart,
But the love in my heart
Shall never depart
I will love you my friend
Till the end.
For friendship to love
Comes down from above
Its course we could hardly endure,
For the sorrows we share
And the deeds that we dare
May divide
But never obscure.

A PROMISE

Mid sorrows around me
To your altar I bring
A garland of roses
Entwined with my ring,
They both shall remind you
Of the joys that are gone
Like the last fading notes
Of the nightingale's song.
A promise I make you,
Mid soft falling tears,
To cherish forever
Our first joyful years
That grew all around us
In spring's early bloom
To fade
And to wither
And perish too soon.

FLORA MACDONALD

Oh my Bonnie Prince, my heart is breaking,
The grass is wet with hail and rain,
The burns over flow
The trees are weeping
The piprock's song flowers over the glen . . .
And you and I must part forever
Oh never more my love to see,
What fate denied was not a nation
But the esteems and love
I felt for thee.
Let the piprocks rise with sad lamentings
And lavrocks sing their weary songs,
Let the burns go dry and mountain streams
Flow on until I die . . .
Let rivers run their cheerless course
Aye until the end of time!
But I swear my lord
For all their tears
They are not as sad as mine.

THE IMAGE

By my window
Near the firelight
Peeping through the purple gloom,
Stands a lady I remember
Eerily standing in my room.
Proud and stately
Though quiet in bearing
Dressed in garments
With shades of dark,
Highly strung of disposition
Her hair is long
And her eyes are black.
A wraith she is
Who comes of lately,
Nightly visits to my room.
Still as proud,
Still as stately
Whispering words
Of death and doom.
All the while the candles flicker
And the fire is warm and bright,
But the cold is overbearing
And the room is dark as night.
Unannounced she pays her visits
While I wait with bated breath,
For she who stands there
In the darkness
Is my image
And my death.

QUIBERON

Leave me here
Amid the roses of Taiwan,
Among the hills of Nesse
To wander amid the gardens of the rising sun.
Leave me to the wave singing surf
That falls on the shores of Lenor
Where the sands of the Moon God lie
All coloured in red and gold,
Glistening like the rubies of the eastern sea
Where the earth and the ocean sleep forever,
And the children of the night
Play among the stars.
Leave me here
And I shall see you again
In Quiberon.

ENVY

Pale ashen cheeks
Lips ruby red,
Dressed for a wedding
Now lying dead.
All those around her
Kneeling to pray
Blessing the death
That took her away.

She walked among men
With her head in the air
With the moon in her eyes
And the sun in her hair.
But her heart was in heaven
And her feet on the ground,
When they robbed her of honour
She made not a sound.

Beauty and grace
But still more of pride,
Two angels from heaven
Walked by her side.
One gave her tears
The other a kiss
With the laughters of heaven
And the sorrows of this.

THE VIRGIN

A virgin from a page did borrow
A tale of love that spoke of sorrow,
When the book was closed
She wondered why
No matter what
She could not cry.
Love today may turn to sorrow
And a lover's kiss
May only borrow
From a tale of long ago
That spoke of summer
On the virgin snow.
But the world was made for pain
So she reads that tale again,
In her heart she feels the beat
Of a tale so sad and sweet,
Some excuse the strings are loose,
The silken cord has made a noose
And from the close knit
Spider's web
A virgin's blood has made it red.

THE TEAR

Oh cry but once
And leave a tear
To glitter on your eye,
That I may gaze upon that face
Whereon that tear did lie.
For that one tear and for me alone
Ah! No greater gift bestow,
That I may say
Before I die
That tear for me did flow.
And when I do
That gift renew
No sweeter flower you gave
But take it quietly
To where I sleep
And leave it on my grave.

THE SEA BED

Oh winds across the ocean!
Oh winds across the sea!
Search for my beloved
And bring her back to me.

Among the coral she is lying
Ten thousand fathoms deep
Upon a bed of whispering shells
She lies asleep.

Tell her I am waiting
All alone and full of grief
Listening to the pounding waves
Breaking on the reef.

Tell her I am crying
As I have cried for years
Standing upon a bleak and lonely shore
Drowned in tears.

BEATRICE

Oh my love, whom I have loved since childhood,
And whom neither God nor man could e'er divide,
Though seldom blessed I did not curse the blood within us
That made you first my cousin and then my bride.

Nor did I condemn the seed that made us one
That flowered within my heart and vein,
I clutched the rose which blossomed within my soul
Both for the pleasures of its perfume and the petals of its pain.

The hidden petal within the rose's stem
Seeks not a field serene where it may grow,
It is born unknown, and to all eyes unseen,
To blossom or to wither in the summer sun or winter snow.

But now alas, our infant dreams have vanished,
With so much pain I watch them fade away,
My only care to be with you always
And with so much love to kiss your tears away.

For I love you now far more than I have loved you
Within that love my heart finds no repose,
Yet do I smile to hide the pain within me
And with all my heart I bless the love I chose.

So now amid the tears that do surround us
Alike to our common blood our eyes may fill,
Still yet to you alone my tears are flowing
And upon your lips with tender kisses still.

BEATRICE – I SEE YOU EVERYWHERE

I see you in every flower that grows
On the face of all that's fair,
In the stars I see your laughing eyes
In the sun I see your hair.
I hear your laughter in the rippling spring
Down the hill where Melfe flows,
And when the tears lie on your cheek
I see them on the rose.
I see you in all the spheres of Heaven
In the soft velvet lights of stars far flung,
Amid the fires of the breaking morning
On golden thrones beneath the sun.
I see you in the changing tides
When the moons of autumn
Cast their silver lights o'er the sleeping land.
I see you in the far off seas
That weep forever,
I hear your whisper in the sand.

RUTH

Ruth has gone with the raven
She flies upon his wings,
Through the dark abysmal night
Condor black she sings.

Through the moonlight silver beam
Among the spheres of heaven
My Ruth flies all alone
Upon the wings of the condor raven.

Beneath the Promethean fires of heaven
Beneath the blood red sky,
Upon the raven's condor wings
My beloved Ruth still flies.

A worm is waiting by her grave
Quietly within his haven,
But my Ruth flies all alone
Upon the wings of the condor raven.

Oh wait for me, my beloved Ruth,
Demented and insane,
Flying upon the raven's condor wing
Crying out to me in vain.

ELEONORA

Sorrowfully amid the lights now fading fast
I lie with death, awaiting at the door,
I see my children in the shadows weeping
And a sound of distant voices I shall hear no more.

And you, whom I have loved, in sorrow standing
Once tears denied, now weeping, I know not why,
For in all these years now fading into the twilight
No witnessing angel ever heard you cry.

But now you weep for you know that I am dying
And by my side the flowers you never gave,
Oh! Bring them to the altar where they may wither
Or leave them as a memorial upon my grave.

Perhaps it is too soon for the shrouds of mourning
Or listen to the bells as best you can
But far better dressed was I in the morning
The day I heard the bells which at our wedding rang.

So now, alas, I take the flowers you give in sorrow,
As I take the tears you shed for me in vain,
The flowers you ever gave to me were born of pity
But the flowers I gave to you were born of pain.

So you may stand there with my children all around you
And mourn for me when I lie among the dead,
Your tears are falling upon my pillow
And the flowers you bring are lying upon my bed.

REPRESSION

Perhaps there is nothing left of life but sorrow
And perhaps there is nothing left to forgive or to forget
What pain there is,
We may postpone
Until tomorrow
But the agony remains with our tears,
So cold and wet.
The sunken ground may bear the weight
Of muffled feet
And the soul may struggle still
With the vanished scenes;
But all the ugly dolls we buried
Ten thousand fathoms deep
Shall arise to play their part
In the theatre of our dreams.
The bubbling cauldron of too much grief
And repressed fears
Boils over
And spills around the furrowed ground
And beneath the shades of night;
And remorseful tears
We may cry and cry
Or laugh without a sound.
Then day by day the ghosts of past regret
Shall come a-haunting
Through these rooms
Once warm and bright,
And when the sun goes down
Upon these tears

So cold and wet
Our dreams shall awaken again to the horrors
Of another night.

TWO EAR-RINGS

My little brother never smiled since mother died
No matter the tales we told,
He would just stare
At a yellow ribbon
And two ear-rings
Made of gold.

His cheeks were pale and white as snow
And his hands were always cold,
But he would just stare
At a yellow ribbon
And two ear-rings
Made of gold.

There were always tear drops in his eyes
And down his cheeks they rolled,
To lie upon a yellow ribbon
And two ear-rings
Made of gold.

Then one day we lost him and we cried
For he was only five years old,
In his little hand
A yellow ribbon
And two ear-rings
Made of gold.

We laid him by his mother's side
And we wept to see him hold
With so much love
A yellow ribbon
And two ear-rings
Made of gold.

THE GRAVE

Stand by her grave
Tear stained eyes
And heavy heart,
The world has passed you by
And the face of Christ is made of stone.
Lay your head upon her tomb
And comfort seek
No finger there shall rise,
To point the way
Or forgiveness find from the dead
We have not slain,
For they have no need
Of our tears and sighs.
Our guilt is beyond the confine of their dreams,
They too walk among the estranged stars
And sleep beneath the poppies
In a foreign field.
For we are but worshippers of an empty tomb,
The lovers of the lost
We shall never find,
They arc but the idols,
The Golden Calf
The dust
Whom God in his anger
Has scattered to the wind.

THE MIRROR

The mirror
And paint,
The wrinkles
And tears,
The fast flowing tide
Of oncoming years;
My young days are over
My hair is now grey
And the joys of my youth
Have all passed away.

Sorrow
And sadness,
The grief
And the pain,
The memories of gladness
I conjure in vain.
Too late for wild fancies
The nights are too long
The morning is over
And my lovers have gone.

ANNABELL

Oh Annabell!
My beloved bride,
Living within the moonlight beam,
Walking alone
By night and day
As in a dream.
Oh my beloved how I love you!
Though your eyes have lost their glow,
Though all your tears
Have turned to ice
And your hair has turned to snow.

Oh Annabell, whom the moon has struck,
And I shall never find
For though you are always with me
You walk one step behind . . .
Like a flower that grows in winter
And withers in the snow
Waiting for the summer
It will never know.

AGE

Tears from her eyes
Down ancient sorrows roll,
As lines
Upon furrowed lines
Play around the soul;
Appetite
Allied to appetite
Still draws a fleeting breath,
That seeks amid the soothing pangs of hunger
A holiday from death.
A withered hand outstretched
Puts out the flickering light
And from the cradling comfort of her bed
Bids her tears goodnight.

LOVE

The wind is so cold
And the rain is so wet
And my memories of you
I cannot forget.
My life
All around me
Is passing away
For the girl that I love
Has left me today.

The wind and the winter
The sun and the rain,
The seasons keep coming
Again and again.
But my heart is no longer
What it was long ago,
For I loved you more dearly
Than you will ever know.

EL DORADO

Two pilgrims
By a wayside inn
And between them stood a shadow
Who pointed to the golden road
That led to El Dorado.
And they with wine
Their cups filled up
And drank to El Dorado
While laughter filled the space between
Those pilgrims and the shadow.
With day gone by
They fell asleep
And with them slept the shadow,
As in their cups
But now in dreams
They dreamt of El Dorado.
And then with dawn
Their dreams were gone
And so alas the shadow
Whose lonely figure can still be seen
On the road to El Dorado.
Both pilgrims
Took up their rags and left
To each his own sweet shadow
Draped in jewels
They never found
On the road to El Dorado.

THE INDIAN

This flag is yours
But the land is mine,
What you give
Is yours to give,
What you take is mine.
The sword upon your mantlepiece
Is the emblem of your race,
The heart it pierced
Was always yours
But the blood alas
Was mine.

MATADOR

The sun
And the sand
The bull
And the ring
The crowds are awaiting
For death to begin.
It comes in the evening
Oriego is dead
The roses are white
But the petals are red.

THE DISMAL SWAMP

Fare ye well my Mary
To Atlanta I must go,
Across the Blue Ridge Mountains
To the sea,
To the valley of the Shenandoah.
By the dismal swamp
I am sleeping,
I can hear the wild goose cry,
In my dreams I see you weeping
In the morning I shall die.
Then bury me deep
By the dismal swamp
And build me a swift canoe
That I may sail
By night and day
To be again with you.

BILLY THE KID

La Punta della Glorietta
Near Sumner
By the Pecos Valley,
They say Pat Garret
Shot Billy the Kid
In a bedroom battle volley.
But Billy was too fast for Pat
Aye for Pat and another four,
The only way the Kid could die
Was if his back was to the door.
For Billy was a legend
And a hero with a gun
No faster draw in all the west
Than Billy at twenty-one.
But he was tired of running
From the law
And from himself,
So that night he put his guns away
At the midnight hour of twelve
And hid them on a shelf.
It was at White Oaks Nevada
A few miles from Santa Fé
That Billy the Kid rode into town
On a warm and sultry day.
For a while he hung around the town
But he was feeling sore
For two hundred eyes
Makes two hundred spies
And another two makes four.

But dammit all
A man must die,
If it comes
Let it come by day,
So he chose a saloon
Predestined by doom
For fate was staring his way.
They will tell you a tale
Of this I am sure
Those eyes that were two hundred and four,
With no guns in his belt
And the way that he felt
With his back that was facing the door.
But Billy the Kid
From fear never hid
So he stood with fate standing by,
But the marshall was waiting
In the darkness debating
With death gleaming dark in his eye.
It came with the sun
Sparkling bright on a gun
It came with his back to the door,
Four shots in his head
And Billy lay dead
With his blood like a flood
On the floor.
La Punta della Glorietta
Near Sumner
By the Pecos Valley,
They say Pat Garret
Shot the Kid
In a bedroom battle volley.

But the darkness tells lies
Making two hundred spies
Taking wings over the dry Pecos Valley.

THE CHILDREN OF SHENANDOAH

Shenandoah
Sweet waters rippling,
Blue Ridge Mountains
Covered in snow.
Wandering winds
Where are my children,
The winds whisper nowhere
While the sweet waters flow.
All around me my children
To awaken the dawn
With soft singing voices
Their first morning song;
The winter has broken
The wild goose has fled
My children around me
Are sleeping in bed.
Oh Shenandoah valley
Soft speaking trees
Covered in foliage
And quiet falling leaves,
Cradle them close
In the dawn of their years
Their soft singing voices
Are singing of tears.

THE CHILD SOLDIERS OF THE SOUTH

Beneath that battlefield of mourning
Beneath the quiet fields of the Shenandoah
In their long grey coats the children are sleeping
In a blanket of cold beneath the fresh virgin snow.

No bugler's alarm shall awake their wild yearning
To arise in the morning their faces aglow,
Their hearts are engraved in a moonlight of sorrow
Beneath the quiet fields of the sweet Shenandoah.

They stood before Sheridan their eyes all ablaze
With that great expectation of children at play,
How little they knew that the sound of the cannon
Was a thunder of death that would take them away.

They came from parade at the first light of dawn
And the smile on their lips was a rosary to God
At the bugler's command they went forth to their glory
To die on the fields of the sweet Shenandoah.

They carried them back from that battle at night
And laid them in rows beneath the dark sky
In their long grey coats it seemed they were sleeping
Like tired little children too weary to cry.

So the chill winds of the winter gave way to the sun
And a perfume of summer blew over the snow
But the south's fading dreams lay buried forever
Beneath the quiet fields of the sweet Shenandoah.

THE SHENANDOAH

In the cold light of dawn when the summer was over
And the first fall of snow was seen on the hills,
Lee with his troops gazed over the valley
While Sheridan and Grant crossed the wide Shenandoah.

They came in their thousands without haste and without fear
With their banners unfurled to the breaking of day,
And the smoke from their cannons at the rear of the field
Rose like a white cloud that faded away.

By midday that valley was covered in carnage
And Grant quit the field like the flight of the crow,
While Sheridan remained to laugh at the slaughter
And the blood of the dying in the cold virgin snow.

In the still of the evening when the light had all gone
And the fires of the living cast their flames o'er the dead,
To the far distant hills the eagles departed
While the Shenandoah River flowed silent and red.

FREEDOM

Paint your face, nigger man,
Paint your black face white,
For them hooded men are on their way
To hang you high this night.

They don't like you, nigger man,
Your skin is too damn black,
And them hooded men are on their way
To tear it from your back.

Go paint your face
And shave your head,
Make sure you act damn white
For them hooded men are on their way
To hang you high this night.

But don't you call them master
Just change your goddamn looks,
Them hooded men that's on their way
Ain't fit to clean your boots.

So go now to your cabin
And paint your black face white,
For them hooded men are on their way
And you will die this night.

But don't you cry, nigger man,
Just paint your black face white,
For them hooded men that's on their way
Will set you free this night.

THE STRANGE TOWN

Denver Colorado
On the road to Santa Fé
A small little town called Sadness
Just one mile and half away.

Now the nights can be real lonely
And the days can be so long
A man has got to rest you know
Before he travels on.

Now that advice came as a whisper
And I swear it was not mine
So I cocked my ears and there it was
I heard it one more time.

Up there in the shades, it said,
You will find a bed tonight
All alone in a nice quiet room
Where you can sleep till light.

Well I was tired and weary
With a weariness strangely dense
A nice quiet room and a lovely bed
Made an awful lot of sense.

So I made my way towards the shades
And there above the door
Was a sign, with "Rooms" in neon lights
Just "Rooms", and nothing more.

Now the doors were made of metal
And the bells were merely chains
The windows made of pebble shells
With criss-cross twisted panes.

I rang the bell which made a sound
So quiet I could hardly hear
As if that house was built on sorrow
And the earth was made of fear.

But goddammit I was weary
And I needed sleep real bad
So I rang, and I rang, then to the door
Came a figure old and sad.

"I am sorry, sir, to keep you waiting,"
He said with solemn tones
In such a way I swear to God
It chilled my flesh and bones.

I mumbled something about a room
"Ah yes! Ah yes! A bed . . .
A single bed in a very quiet room
A single bed," he said.

Within the hallway beyond the door
I saw the stairs rise high
As if they led to eternal gloom
Where only the dead would lie.

But oh my God! I was dozing fast,
And to nothing else I gave
One single thought, but a place to sleep
If need be in the grave.

"Sir," the figure said to me,
"I am sure you will find it best
To come and dine with us
Then you may take your rest."

"Don't you worry about the price,
Sit down awhile and eat.
It will not take me very long
To prepare you a fleshy meat."

"Ah no! It will not take me long
I swear it will not take me long.
Just sit down and eat with us
It will not be very long."

It seemed that I was dreaming
For they were thousands beyond the door
Waiting for a bed to sleep
Just a bed and nothing more.

But to all who came the figure said,
"Please sit down and dine."
And on each plate was the fleshy meat
And a bottle of blood red wine.

Every mouthful tasted sweet
Every mouth was red
With that soft and fleshy meat
With that wine so red.

I heard young children crying
I heard the figure laugh,
"One more portion for the beast,"
He cried to the kitchen staff.

From out of darkness into darkness
Through the lonely streets I fled,
Past the deep and open graves
Past a thousand beds.

Denver Colorado
On the road to Santa Fé
A small little town called Sadness
Just one mile and a half away.

Perhaps I was only dreaming
Or perhaps it was really true
But I swear to God if you reach that town
Just you drive right through.

NASHVILLE TENNESSEE

Too much heartache
Too much pain
And I know the road is long
But I must keep on moving
Just keep moving on.

I am going home to Nashville
In the heart of Tennessee
To the place I left
Where I was born
Sweet Nashville Tennessee.

There's nothing here to keep me
And nothing to leave behind
But a load of misery in my heart
And troubles on my mind.
I've tasted all there is to taste
And I'm bleeding to death inside
I just want to find a place worth keeping
A place where I can hide.

So I am going home to Nashville
In the heart of Tennessee
To the place I left
Where I was born
Sweet Nashville
Tennessee.

KHAYYAM

Khayyam drinks deep of bitter wine
While the poet falls asleep
And beside the muse's bed a lion
A solemn vigil keeps.
A verse of purple poems are read
Which fall on iron ears
So heaven opens wide its gates
To the attentive listening spheres,
Then gods of far away distant times
Come once again to reign
And all the world lies down to weep
The poet's woeful pain.
Satan rides out on a headless mule
With a twin edged sword of pride
While Christ sits down on a golden throne
With Mahomet by his side.
Then a hundred million blades of grass
Awake to a withered flower,
Its song a perfect hymn of praise
Beyond the poet's power.
For such a song do angels sing
A music so divine
That even Omar from his eastern tower
Puts down his cup of wine.

THE SIOUX

Quiet flowing waters
Pebbles of gold,
Blood spattered flowers
Stories of old,
Valleys and mountains
Covered in snow,
Bright coloured tents
By the sweet Shenandoah.
Grass growing high
Flowers in spring,
Wind trembling trees
Petals that sing,
So much of nature
Still yet divine
As proud as the eagle
As strong as the pine.
Tents in the desert
Horse and canoe,
Land of the warrior
Land of the Sioux,
Now God-forsaken
Robbed of your land
They have taken your tents
And left you the sand.

THE CANOE

Down through the misty waters gliding
Draped in deathly blue,
Sails the Lady of the Marshes
In her white canoe.
Through the flamingo's haven
Past the heron's nest
Where the birds of all the forest
Come to take their rest.
Oh where are you sailing to
In the dead of night
Beneath that sky so red?
"I am sailing to the Shenandoah
To gather up my dead."
Pale blue eyes overcast
Her cheeks as white as snow,
"I must gather up my children
By the banks of the Shenandoah."
High above the stars are weeping
For the lady draped in blue
Gliding through the misty waters
In her white canoe.

THE YOUTH

It was not strange
Or was it,
When we were very young
To sing the songs we thought our own
To find them already sung.
Down the left wing alley-ways
In Bohemian dress awry
To catch a glimpse of melody
That could make us laugh or cry . . .
The last fond kiss
Ere youth be gone
The flight from love and home,
Around the pole four hundred times
But we were not alone.
Five hundred thousand banners flew
Above the turrets of a single sky
To see the last ten thousand tears
That fell from a single eye.
We lit Promethean fires
To warm the chill within
But the wine was gone
And the summer too
And the joys of thoughtless sin.
So we turned to face the demons
But our hearts were cold and years
Of singing songs and melodies
Had perished with our tears.

CHILDHOOD

All my children around me
From the past of my childhood
To remind me of the love
My father denied.
A memory of fair fields
The grove
And the woodlands
And a stool by the fire
Where so often I cried.
Forlorn would I wander
Through the forest alone
Though my father behind me
Would stroll without care.
No kiss on my cheek
No father's embrace
No hand to unruffle
As wind through my hair.
So little was given
Yet so much did I give
Amid the faults of my childhood
He could not forgive.
Yet I though a child
From the depths of my fear
Would take a toy to my heart
And afford it a tear.
So now do I gather
My children around me
To banish the dreams
Of my childhood at last.

And when we return
From the field
And the woodland
A kiss on their lips
When their pleasures have passed.

THE SPECTRE OF MARRIAGE

The spectre of the altar
Through midnight hours of fear
A vision of ten thousand oaths
Come whispering to the ear.
O'er a pathway paved to ancient halls
Through mansions dimly lit
An audience of ten thousand tears
With pain and sorrow sit.
And through the vision of their dreams
A ghostly pen proscribes
Too many laws they must not break
Or even dare describe.
Then o'er the solemn guests of dust
A webbed spider weaves
A net of flimsy moss around
A million withered leaves.
And then the final curtain drawn
O'er the light that fades forever
A demon white with pain and age
Puts a ring upon their finger.
Applause breaks upon the scene
Like thunder across the sea
But they who now applaud the most
Are those from chains set free.
The vision fades in the light of dawn
As it did ten thousand years
Amid the oaths of many smiles
And twenty million tears.

THE FAMILY

Flickering pictures on television
Casting shadows upon the wall
Long blue curtains with shades of purple
To shut out the light before darkness falls.

A family gathering of perfect strangers
Priceless moments passing by
Silence is the only word unspoken
A sitting-room ceiling is the only sky.

Children gazing at their parents
Parents gazing at the screen
An old man awakes from boredom sleeping
Dreaming of the faces he has never seen.

A voice from somewhere speaks of something
Someone listens but cannot hear
Silence is the only cross worth bearing
Love the only thing to fear.

Dinner is over and the family wanders
Each to their separate rooms until the sun's retire
Vacant houses without a family
Empty houses without a fire.

THE SCOLDING

The hand upraised
Threatens
Then strikes
The child can only cry,
He does not even wonder
Nor ask his father why.

About his feet
His little toys
Are left to play alone,
He dries the tear drops on a baby doll
And then he dries his own.

His father
Puts the child to sleep
And breathes a heavy sigh
Then going to his room
To read
He hangs his head
To cry.

THE GARDEN

When sorrows around me are pressing
Too deep for my heart to suppress
I wander amid the flowers in my garden
And a rose to my lips I caress.

It reminds me of the days that are over
Of the joys that were mine, and your smile
That so often restored the bright sunshine
And tempered my grief for awhile.

But it returns, amid the shades, and the shadows
That spread o'er my soul like a mist
To awaken the sadness within me
And the tears I cannot resist.

I listen to your voice though a whisper
Oh that sound I gladly would hear!
To feel if but once your sweet finger
To dry if it could but one tear.

But I know you have left me forever
To wander in this garden forlorn
And my tears shall flow on like a river
To the source from which they were born.

EXECUTION OF DANTON

It was sufficient for him to catch a glimpse
Of the last green field
And where the mist appears
The last red rose,
Sadly he hears the applause
That no pity yields
And the cries that from the pleb arose.
When he was a child he dreamed of victory
Upon the land or on some ship at sea
It came from out a platform
In a new republic
Amid the terrors he could not bear to see.
So now for France he weeps
But not in sorrow
As now to France he gives
Both heart and soul.
The flags are waving
But not in victory
The blade is ready
And the drums begin to roll.

ELIZABETH AND ESSEX

Had she ruled you less
And loved you more
She would not rue this day
To take from this its greatest gift
That tears cannot repay.
What ambition rules
The heart must rue
As Elizabeth rues the hour
That saw proud Essex shame her pride
To die within the tower.
For love o'erthrows ambition's creed
And thrones around it rock
The day dear Essex undid his chains
To die upon the block.
And she a queen now rules alone
Who once a crown could share
She sits alone on a golden throne
As cold as a widow's chair.

THE YELLOW THEATRE

The footlights play upon the theatre of life
And corroding age trails its ancient gown,
And through the revolving mirrors of joy and strife
We are sometimes the hero and sometimes the clown.

For the heart clings to the motley parts we play
Beneath the tinkling bells of happier themes,
But the applause once loved is fading away
And the lights are out in the theatre of our dreams.

Across mountain paths that youth denotes
As merely pathways that span the bridge of time,
In decaying age are no longer hilly slopes
But mountains to the sky too high to climb.

The hero of the plot must play his part
As an ageing player in marble halls,
But when the music swells and the curtain falls
The heroes of the plot are the tinkling bells.

For therein lies the tragedy of the play
In the distant memories of life's most cherished themes,
But the author of the plot has passed away
And all that is left of life
Is the yellow theatre of our dreams.

NOTHING

The art of the great poets
Lay in their ability
To create from nothing
Something that was not there
And put in its place
Something that was.

BYRON'S FAREWELL TO ENGLAND

Farewell,
Farewell,
My native shore is fading into the mist.
Farewell the loves I leave behind
And the lips that I have kissed.
Farewell my father's ancient home,
Farewell my mother's tears,
My native shore is fading fast
Where out the mist appears.
Forlorn before me I see the waves
The ocean's mighty swell,
The lighthouse stark beyond the reef
And the sailor's warning bell.
I hear the warring winds that blow
Through the sail of the towering mast,
The crimson sunlight's pallid glow
Where the skies are overcast.
From England's verdure vales I quit
Both my loves and ill repute
That they who knew me least of all
May now my faults impute.
Let others seek in foreign climes
The refuge they would seek
From the shallow confines of their dreams
Oh mine are far too deep.
But deeper still than the ocean's swell
Are the tears that within me pour,
Oh fare ye well my native land,
Farewell my native shore.

DOMINIC

If I am what I am
Then let it be,
For nothing upon earth
Was as foul to me
As the coward who smiles
For fear of the brave
And cries on his pillow
For fear of the grave.
There are no pavilions
We raise to the dead
Who fought their last battle
From their trenches in bed.
If courage there was
It was not in the mind
The lions of Judah
Were attacked from behind.
With glory attending
I laughed at the rule
To smile with the idiot
And bear with the fool.
If there is a heaven
Let it be here
And cursed be the coward
Who gained it by fear.
For over that mountain
I covered my eyes
For fear of the angel
And the shame of disguise,
Their anger is pride

Their ignorance is bliss
With future damnation
And mockery in this.

THE DEVIL'S NIGHT TIME FAIR

Eliza Meeton and the parson's wife,
The grocer and the mayor,
All together in a single file
To the night time devil's fair.
From Mearly Meed and Marstons Hall
From the marshes near Dunoon,
From the lower hills where the waters fall
Beneath the light of the crescent moon.
All together and the fair begins
First with music
Then with hymns,
A burning bush and the skies are red
The trees are bare
And the owls have fled.
Tiptoe dancers around and around,
Children staring without a sound,
A fiddler fiddles on a single string
The men are dancing
And the women sing.
Time to eat and they all sit down
To a very fleshy meat
And a very red wine,
A cry is heard like a dying child
Their lips are smeared
And their eyes are wild.
The night is late
It is time to go,
Some ride fast
And some ride slow

But all are flying before the light
Breaks the spell of a very dark night.
Eliza Meeton and the parson's wife,
The grocer and the mayor,
All together in a single file
From the devil's night time fair.

SAINT ANTHONY'S WELL

The hills of Saint Margaret are covered in sleet
And dark hangs the mist over King Arthur's Seat,
The valleys are silent and night comes awake
As the last birds of evening fly over the lake.

A shepherd comes down all alone with his flock
As the cold winds of winter shriek out from the rock,
He listens with wonder to the sound of the bell
That comes from the cup in Saint Anthony's Well.

He takes the chill water and drinks to the name
Of God and his angels and Saint Anthony's fame,
The sky is now brighter he drives through the dell
To the murmur of silence and the toll of the bell.

THE COMPANIONS

Oh destined am I
To walk through these valleys
Mid the fertile green fields
That lie by the vale.
Oh where are they now
My once dear companions
Who joyfully marked time
In our school days at Yale?
How bravely we matched
Our endeavours with nature
To endure what the wise
To the brave would deny.
The applause of the senate
We gladly ignored
But the praise of the mild
We endured with a sigh.
The pleasures of love
Were as dear to us then
As the pleasure of dreams
Are as dear to me now.
Oh how we longed
To change our condition
To foil with the sword
And toil with the plough.
But they came in their turn
Both the war and the field
And labour gave way
To the sweat of our tears
To break both our hearts

And the will of our fathers
To sever forever
From those last pleasant years.
So now through these valleys
I walk in my sorrow
To dream of my youth
And companions all gone,
And the winds of the past
Through the leaves of my childhood
Seem to blow their sweet praises
Through the tears of my song.

FAIRIES

Oh come and dance with the fairy folk
There is dancing in the square
And long white skirts
And big black boots
And ribbons in their hair.
Come and sing with the fairy folk
A wild and merry tune
With a fiddle
And a flute
And a big big drum
And a hymn to the man in the moon.
For the sun goes up
And the sun comes down
And we have danced by night and day.
But who will dance
When the music stops
And the fairies fly away?

THE TREMBLING CITY

Listen all ye passers by
Heed well to what I say,
Ere night comes down
Flee this town
Before the end of day.
Do not tarry
But fly, oh fly,
Stay not here awhile,
Too many demon witches haunt
This so called Royal Mile.
Oh many the tales
That I could tell
Of sorrows and despair,
Of headless queens
And armless knights
Of dreadful Burke and Hare,
Of Sweeney Todd
And Brother Claude,
Who burn in endless fires,
Saint Mary's Street
And Arthur's Seat
And the wynd they call Blackfriars.
Their very names are legion
They cast an awful spell
That does not come from heaven
But from the fires of hell.
For sorrow creeps in every close
In every street and wynd
Flee I say, oh flee,
And leave all else behind.

Within this shoppe
This parchment bears
The stamp of evil lore
And he who wrote
Having written once
Can write to you no more.
For here within at midnight sharp
There glides the phantom cat
That once so many years ago
Sat on Queen Mary's lap.
It creeps around the corners dark
Still crying for its queen
And when the moon is awful full
With her he can be seen.
Still sitting upon her queenly lap
And she without her head
Still singing songs
And lullabies
For her lovers who are dead.
So listen all ye passers by,
Heed well to what I say,
Ere night comes down
Flee this town
Then bend your knees to pray.
For lo!
Oh lo!
The night comes down
Oh hear her cries of pity
The palace lights
Are out!
Are out!
Dark lies the trembling city.

THE EARL OF MORAY

Let Scotland boast
And England toast
The lions
That above us flurry,
But none so brave
That could enslave
The bonnie Earl of Moray.
Let history page
Its greatest age
Where none but the rats may scurry,
For none so great
That could emulate
The gallant Earl of Moray.
The muse may frown
On a Scottish crown
And the poets
To their graves may hurry,
But no tears so sweet
As on the cheeks
Of the bonnie Earl of Moray.
For he was loved
So well beloved
But never a maid would curry,
But many a maiden broke her heart
For the bonnie Earl of Moray.
A traitor's hand
Did thus command
With neither care nor worry,
The dues were paid

To the knave who slayed
Our gallant Earl of Moray.
The English rose
That sweetly grows
No foreign hand shall sully,
But none so sweet o'er the Scottish moors
As the grave
Of the Earl of Moray.

THE LIGHTS OF FIFE

From the Banks of Dalmeny
I gaze over Fife
Where the lights from its shore
Remind me of life.
Too late to appear
Too soon to depart
While the thoughts in my mind
Are breaking my heart.
Over many a land
I have wandered at will
But the Banks of Dalmeny
Are dear to me still.
For when the pale moon
Beams on my strife
I see in my tears
The sweet lights of Fife.
Best loved are the stars
That vanish with dawn
As the love in our hearts
When passion has gone . . .
The land we have loved
Through sorrow and pain
The hands we have held
But hold not again.
So much then of grief
Has passed through my life
To leave me a pilgrim
From the sweet lights of Fife.
'Tis all but a dream

As I gaze o'er the wave
For the Banks of Dalmeny
Is but a cloud o'er my grave.

SILHOUETTES

Black portraits
Of trees
And hills,
Silhouettes
Of birds
Against a crimson sky,
Snow flake swans
Still awake
Gliding
With so much grace
Across a cardboard lake.
Heavenly hands
A painting traces
Upon a canvas
Of days and night,
A silhouette of black
Upon the silver twilight
And a crimson portrait
Of the night.

THE FEAST

Demon dancers long deceased
Making ready for the feast
While an infant baby cries
A fresh new victim for the beast.

Frenzy fills the dancing master
Bidding the demons to dance faster
And they in dread obedience dance
While the devil applauds their master.

Moonlight stealing through the trees
Silver sandals upon the leaves
One foot west and one foot east
No one comes and no one leaves.

Worms there are who come and go
Lifeless flowers unperfumed grow
And all around the hellish ground
The pale moon paints a purple glow.

Faster and faster dance the dancers
Before the worms that make no answer
Waiting for the crumbs to fall
From the table of their master.

Quiet the wilderness with the approach of dawn
Wearily from afar the lark's first song
A wild goose flies to its very edge
Then like a ghost it flies anon.

Till at last the infant sleeps
Clutching the soul it cannot keep
Watchful demons wait around
Where only angels kneel and weep.

Dawn has broken in the east
While the forest hides its feast
The worms are quivering o'er the soil
Feeding on the crumbs left by the beast.

THE BED

For me the sun begins to set
Night's shadows gently fall
My life has run to eventide
And sleep does softly call
I shall not rest in voluptuous silk
No pillow of cloth shall hold my head
The flowers alone shall mark my place
The earth shall be my bed.

CROSS

The cheerless morning is breaking
Betwixt the sun and the falling moon,
But the darkness strikes the evening
Then strikes again at noon.
There is a strange uneasy feeling
Among the fools who most applaud
The usurping thrones of angels driven
Into the broken arms of God.
Where once a weak and weary youth
With ageless wisdom wept
Upon a virgin's sinless heart
A dark appointment kept.
Upon a hill which turned to flames
Beneath a blushing sky
With a crown of piercing thorns a King
Prepares His bed to die.
The eagle awaits the breaking day
From its nest of pride and regal home
To watch the burning crosses burn
Along the Appian way to Rome.
But all alone in Sion
Amid the fires of the dying flame
A virgin maiden takes her child
Into her arms again.
She does not look for comfort
His blood is on the bark
Her tears are falling into the dust
Her kisses are in the dark.

KING DAVID'S LAMENT

Oh Absalom,
Oh Absalom,
They have left you on the field,
Among the dead whereon the sun
Shines bright upon your shield.
The stars of heaven twinkle on
Your face now pale in death
Across which blows a sorry wind
To hold you in its breath.
Oh Absalom,
Oh Absalom,
By your campfires burning bright,
No watchful sentries stand around
To guard your tent this night.
For an angel of the Lord has weighed
So well the day I sinned
To make of you a child of wrath
To scatter to the wind.
What cursed fault was mine alone
Was levied to your head
Jehovah's ransom was heavily priced
With innocent blood so red.
Oh Michael Angel, my sin forgiven,
Give me back my son,
That I may hold him once again
Oh Absalom,
My son, my son.

CALVARY

Oh mighty cross of Christ foreboding
Shadowed darkness on a hill
See it spreading
Ever spreading,
Oh face of Christ
So quiet and still.
Blood draped phantoms
Gaping high
Upon a bleak and angry sky,
Waiting
Oh forever waiting
For the Son of God
To die.
Cast across the Judaean desert
Sweeping o'er the Aegean sea
Hear Him whimper
God of heaven
Take Him from that spiteful tree.
Silent now
Forever silent
Sunlight breaking across the sky
Stark against the bright horizon,
Oh Son of God
Why did You die?

DEATH

Death
A button
A comb
A dress on a hanger . . . torn
And memories,
Memories
And memories,
The lengthful days
Made longer by the sun
Whose light can never cheer
Nor warmth can ever warm.
Oh that it could end,
The long, long day!
And sleepless nights
Made restful by repose!
O could these tears to heaven flow!
This heart now broken die.

FEAR

Run!
Run!
Run!
There is no place to go
You can make it even faster
But you had better make it slow.
You're up too tight,
You're breaking down,
There is nothing up there ahead,
The traffic lights have turned to green
But the lights are in your head.
There is a road somewhere to nowhere
You can see it through the rain,
You can run
And run
As best you can
But you'll still come back again.
The thing to do
Is take it easy
It will pay you in the end,
Just turn around
And walk away
There is no one there, my friend.

THE BEAST

Oh come my friends and dance with me,
There is a devil out there tonight,
Leave your wives until another time
For too soon it will be light.

Oh come my friends and sing with me,
The beast is at the gate,
Leave your chores until another time
For the hour is very late.

Oh come my friends and laugh with me,
For the hound is baying the moon,
Leave your prayers until another time
For the dawn will be breaking soon.

Oh come my friends and cry with me,
The master is at the feast,
Leave your tears until another time
For tonight is the night of the beast.

MADNESS

Hidden voices from out of madness
From the source of fear and sadness,
From the unconscious fears that dwell
Within each man and child as well.
Masks that hide the other face
The rot within as silk and lace
The masks of Adam,
The masks of Eve,
The first born child from the covering leaf.
Dreams from out the great taboo
The only lie that seems so true
No reason breaks on the heart to cry
The fear gives way but cannot die.
Every shadow and every gloom
Are but dreams within the womb,
The infant seed to manhood grown
The ancient soil and his native home.
The thoughtless finger a name would trace
Upon each lip a mother's face
And there a last fond kiss impress
Upon his bride in her wedding dress.
The future haven that fears inspire
Too soon will perish with man's desire,
The listening ear to the voice within
The voice of Oedipus or original sin.

THE FUNERAL

Oh mists of the morning rising,
Oh toll of a thousand bells,
Faces gaping like the demon
Through the windows of a thousand hells.
Oh hurry her to burial
Through the curious weepless throng.
There is a place where men lie weeping
And no one gone.
Oh birth of a thousand mornings
Set in a single sun,
Like the birth of a thousand children
Where there are none.

THE INSISTENT BELL

On ticks the clock,
On tolls the bell,
With no account of heaven
And no account of hell,
Just a never ending now
That shall go on forever
What time there is
Has ended now
Forever and forever.
The midnight hour at midnight stops
Though we cling to its hands forever
To and fro it peals . . .
From side to side its knell . . .
The clock may tick but cannot stop
The toll of the insistent bell.

NIGHT

Silence bewitched by the moon
And night
Without colour
And without light.
Darkness from out of darkness
Into darkness falls
And madness from out the moonlight comes
To paint with silver moonbeams bright
The tormented face of purple night.

THE LAST ROSE OF SUMMER

Wind trembling trees
Their leaves are shedding
The summer is over
And the winter is spreading
Its shadows so long
O'er the vale golden hill
Where a last rose of summer
Is blooming there still.
Oh grow summer rose,
With the blackbirds around you,
May a ray from the sun
Your blossom renew.
Oh sad as I am
I long to be near you
And drop all my tears
On your petals like dew.
With you I would cherish
Life's early bloom
And the last rays of summer
That will perish so soon.
So now to my heart
I press you forever
Oh last summer rose
We are withering together.

HELL

There are amid those far-off regions
Spheres
Unknown to men,
Where angels dwell in perpetual gloom
An eternal kingdom,
Silent space,
Wholly quiet
Where demons feed on woeful grief
In perennial sorrow;
Men dispute
But the stars are still
And angels turn from awful woe
In perfect stillness.

AURORA

Saffron Aurora break bright o'er the dawn,
Come forth from your bed
The winter has gone,
The ice on the tree has melted away
Summer has broken
'Tis the sweet month of May.
See the green field
How it awaits your arising
The first tint of red
Across the horizon,
A silhouette of birds
Perched on the tree
Are singing their songs
To the sweet month of May.
Flowers of the spring
Their perfumes have shed
The leaves of the forest
Are turning your bed.
Oh saffron Aurora,
Proud queen of the dawn,
The summer is waiting
And the winter has gone.

THE DAWN

Dark,
But darker still
The dim lit places,
Where o'er the pallid field
The pale moon glows,
Cold to the shrub
A chilling finger traces,
Cold to the dewlands
As cold as the winter snow.
Bracken and bush
In hues of darkness,
Branch and leaf
The trees have shed,
Aye the leaves once golden
In withering piles asleep,
Even the laburnum
Its yellow leaves has shed.
Cold,
But colder still
The landscape distant
Athwart the skyline's distant shore.
Cold the stars
That peer persistent,
Cold the earth
The sunless moor.
But soon the spring
In crimson robes attired
The misty fields will dress
In flimsy moss,

Then the sun,
The warm Apollo,
The golden warrior
The bridge of dawn shall cross.

THE WINDS

Listen to the summer breeze
Sighing softly through the trees
Murmuring quietly,
And oh so light,
Like children whispering in the night.
Listen to the west wind blow
O'er the ice cold winter snow,
Moaning sadly
As though to weep,
Like children crying in their sleep.
Listen to the north east gale
Shrieking through the mist and hail,
Like the mad
Who seek in vain
Their children dying in the rain.
Listen to the autumn breeze
Moving listless o'er the leaves
Tired of winter
Coming soon,
Like children sleeping in their tomb.
Listen to the winds that blow
Ask them sometimes where they go
But the winds no answer gave . . .
To some infant cradle
Or ancient grave.

THE DREAM

Oh bring me wine
When I awake
And a rose
When I am dead,
And from its stem
Take out the thorn
That in my heart once bled.
Then come with poppies
Blooming wild
And leave them where I sleep,
Whereon the unperfumed petals dew
Are tears like mines so deep.
For twilight long
The dream shall be
Around the vanished scene,
Where flowers are only memories
And love is but a dream.

REMEMBER

If you should remember me
Remember only this
These tears
Were my greatest joy
I seal them
With a kiss.
I never fled from sorrow
As children flee the dark
I crushed the rose
But took its thorn
And pressed it to my heart.
Pride I admired
But despised its pain,
Draped in blood
The flag unfurled
Above the laughter
Of all the kingdoms,
Above the tears
Of all the world.
God's time I did not waste
Nor did he waste mine
Despair I drank
To the very dregs
It is a most sweet wine.

THE ONE WAY ROAD

There is a road called Paradise Road
It's fast on a single lane,
Heroin streets
And poppy fields
Sunshine in the rain.
It's never dark along that road
Neon lights all the way
And many a pilgrim travelling light
Has reached it in a day.
There is a music shop on every corner,
Stop there if you can
It's always good to hear a woman singing
Especially if she's a man.
Don't you worry if there is no one listening
It's very hard to tell
Why some folk love to dance in heaven
And some to dance in hell.
Just you keep your mind on driving,
You're a million miles from home,
You can cry if you like on someone's shoulder
Or you can cry alone.
Don't you bother about the weather man
He says the weather's fine
Champagne soon in a purple glass
And a bottle of blood red wine.
It's bright lights now all the way to summer
Starry eyes
And a virgin bride,
And up above the moon is laughing

At least on the other side.
Just take it nice and easy now
Don't fret
Or get up tight,
Just one more pretty place to sleep
One more bed tonight.
Keep your fingers on the wheel
God, you're doing well,
On a one way road that leads to heaven
On a single lane to hell.

NOW

There is no past
Nor future
That is not now
Forever present
Always here.
No place to go
No place to run
Just a crippled hand outstretched
And a distant drum,
The tired
The weak
And the weary.
Meanwhile the book
And the bell,
No other world but this
And no other hell.

THE CITY OF APPAL

Every print and every picture
Every painting on the wall
Seem to point with accusing fingers
At a portrait down the hall
Of a lady young and pretty
But with eyes bereft of pity,
And behind her lay the city
Where I met her in the fall.
But for all my vain endeavours
No more than this can I recall.
Every print and every picture
Every painting on the wall
Seem to whisper to each other
Down the corridors of the hall.
Where a candle's flickering flame
Casts a shadow over all
And the dread drear world of darkness
Takes possession over all,
And within my heart now beating
There comes a voice repeating,
Repeating and repeating
There is nothing to recall.
Every object and every subject,
Every statue large and small,
Seem to call to each other
Like those paintings down the hall,
As if by their insistence
And my own persistence
They could make me ponder and recall

While the midnight hour of darkness strikes
From a timepiece down the hall.
And my heart keeps on repeating
There is nothing there at all
Till at last my mind in dreariness
And my soul oppressed by weariness
Seeks to find an answer
In the prayers I would recall.
But a voice within the prayer
Speaks of sorrow and despair
And the grief that still awaits me
Beyond that spiral winding stair
Of such things I have forgotten,
That lie buried and forgotten,
That are better left forgotten
In those depths they call despair.
Every print and every picture
Every painting on the wall
Bears a strange resemblance
To that lady down the hall
In whose eyes there shone no pity
Though most young and very pretty,
But her resemblance to those figures
Is the strangest thing of all,
And behind her still that city
Where I met her in the fall.
From that city drowned in madness
Where naught else but sadness
Comes to the mind as darkness
To reproach and to appal,
Till the soul's endurance spent
Into hell is darkly sent

To discourse with prints and pictures
And with paintings on the wall
Until the dread drear world of madness
Takes possession over all,
And the dead from out their graves
Return to the city they call Appal.

THE NEGRO WARRIORS

By their campfires at night
The negroes are singing
The songs they once sang
When their children were free.
Oh how they long
For the land of their fathers
To lie with their women
Beneath the sycamore tree.

With the sun in decline
And their masters still sleeping
Their numbers reduced
By the sabre and gun,
With dreams of tomorrow
And tears to their keeping,
A prey to their fears
Ere the slaughter began.

Beneath the stars in the sky
And quiet all around them
Their stirrings but dreams
As they linger at home.
Silent the tears
That fall on their pillow,
As silent as the dawn
That about them had blown.

With its cold light upon them
They awake to the drum
To the sound of the bugle
And the screech of the gun,
Before them the slaughter
Beneath them the snow
Around them the valleys
Of the sweet Shenandoah.

For death came with the dawn
In the voice of the cannon
In the shrieks of the shell
And the screams of the dying,
How little they knew
Of their dreams of the past
That death was the key
That would free them at last.

For on angel bright wings
From their beds they arise
To greet the new morning
With the sun in their eyes.
Their chains are all broken
At last they are free
To lie with their women
Beneath the sycamore tree.

THE FEAR OF LOSS

Oh for a lodging from the cares and the fears
A place in the darkness to water our tears,
A palace of dreams surrounded in moss
From the pleasures of loving and the fears of its loss.

For nothing is sure to the love-broken heart
Save the last hour of death that drives us apart,
A hope may still linger too soon to dissolve
In the hopes of the future we cannot resolve.

Let all men assemble to discuss in the sun
Mid the present that passes and the future to come
Let heaven ordain that earth is a cross
For the proof of our loving is in the fear of its loss.

The minstrel may sing a song to his love
As she stands by her bed as pure as a dove,
She may smile in her joy but sorrow will come
When the candles are out at the birth of her son.

For the curse of the falcon is warm on the claw
That clings to its bait all blooded and raw,
And though it should fall 'twill fall yet alive
While the falcon flies home to the sound of its cries.

So marry away to your pleasures and bliss
To the pleasures of heaven and the pleasures of this,
But no man on earth may temper the cross
That awaits him in loving and the fears of its loss.

CALVINISM

The rose is no longer really red
Nor the pink and purple heather
The day the sun from heaven fled
When Calvin changed the weather.
No Christ
No Cross
Nor the Immaculate
At the road where the crossroad bends,
Just some fellows homeward late
From a market place of friends.
All has changed in the afternoon
To each man his own sad burden,
The day Christ left his mother's womb
When Calvin came to London.
And dimmed all earth in every season
And dim the sun forever
When all men lost both faith and reason
In the Calvin day feasts of November.

THE WARRIOR

He stood on high above other men
Far more a god and man,
Raised apart
With a warrior's heart
In the year of Kubla Khan
But his horse lay grazing,
And his spear,
His shield and scabbard too,
And in its sheath his dagger's teeth
Lay rusting in the morning dew.
And rusting too his sword of steel
His iron heart and will,
The pasturing steed
Replaced the deed
That proposed but could not fill . . .
A dream of warriors that come by night
By his tent where the rivers ran,
So he fled the field
That could not yield
To the dreams of Kubla Khan.
They sought him out in his evening flight
Where the wild flamingoes fly
And on his face lay not a trace
Of the coward about to die.
He bore no arms
Nor held his shield
To protect his breast from death,
But just a prayer they could not share
With his last and only breath.

And legend built a temple where
His sword lay red with rust
And on his grave
There lay a praise
In tainted words of dust:
'Here lies the mighty warrior's heart . . .
Far more a god than man,
Let no man praise this warrior's grave
For fear of Kubla Khan'.
And many a warrior halts his steed
And bowing down to pray
For he who left his scabbard bare
And flung his sword away.
And closely by there runs a stream
They say since the world began,
That flows and glows
Where the tamarand grows
By the grave of the Kubla Khan.

THE POET'S MISTRESS

Hold my hand in yours
And sing to me of death
For love is listening to your song
With bated breath.
Let me not hear of happier days
Amid flowers which never die
But sing to me a sadder song
That I may cry.
Then shall you remember
These tears as dew drops wet
Which throughout life's dying stream
You shall not forget.
The sweeter still the music
And sweeter still the song
You will conceive of me
Some future day
When I am gone.

HUSH LITTLE CHILD

Hush little child for your mother is sleeping,
Leave her to sleep for your mother is sad,
Share in her dreams that she may be dreaming
And pray for a smile that she may be glad.
Bright vestments at night the trees are adorning
The fields are as white as the fresh virgin snow,
That lie of the leaves that fell in the morning
And cover the earth in wanting and woe.
So hush little child for your mother is weeping,
The winter is making your mother so sad,
And see, by your bed your father is sleeping
And dreaming at last that your mother is glad.
Far sweeter now the flowers of the morning
To gentle lines that lie on her brow
Come with your sleep for the morning has broken
And pray where your mother is happier now.

SHENANDOAH

Oh sweet Shenandoah
Red river of sorrow,
What pen may describe
Your beauty but mine,
For I have conceived
Your likeness forever
And made you a symbol
Of all that's divine.
Though Melfe I loved
I loved as a bride
Who was esteemed by her lover
Who flowers by her side,
So little of that
Was I ever to know
When I dreamt of your waters,
Oh sweet Shenandoah.
For what I conceive
Is mine to conceive
What no man may claim
Less 'tis to deceive
For through it there runs
A sadness divine
And the sound of your tears
Are as tearful as mine.
So flow to your source
You red rippling waters
Spread over a course
With your sons and your daughters.
Though unknown to my ears
I long for your streams
And the sound of your tears
That spreads over my dreams.

ARNHEM

To you!
To you!
Dear Arnhem brings
Flowers of summer and flowers of spring,
And when the rose is in its bloom
Arnhem brings it to your room.
Arnhem!
Arnhem!
Young and fair
Oh so tall with golden hair,
Eyes of a deep celestial blue
Arnhem so in love with you.
For you alone he ever wanders
Among the tulip fields of Flanders
Searching for a tulip blue
To bring to God and then to you.
To bring to you his lady fair
With your long ringed golden hair
In whose eyes he could not know
The budding thorns of pain and woe.
Oh! Arnhem,
Arnhem!
Stay away from your lady fair this day
In whose hand the rose in bloom
Alas is withering upon her tomb.
For you!
For you!
He ever wanders
Among the poppy fields of Flanders,
Searching for a poppy blue
To bring to God
And then to you.

RED CHERRIES

Bring me red cherries in the summer
Wild strawberries in the spring
And fill my plate with golden grapes
And fill my cup with wine,
And when the feast is over
In seasons out of time
Bring me red roses in the summer
White roses in the spring.
And leave them by the cypress,
The fir tree and the pine,
And bring me no more golden grapes
And bring me no more wine,
But come with hymns and orisons
And sing to me a song
That you may remember while I am with you
And forget me when I am gone.

THE FLIGHT

Oh tell me young soldier as you fly in retreat
A place in Atlanta where a soldier may sleep,
For I am lost and confounded and no place to go
As Sherman lays waste o'er the wide Shenandoah.

I beg you my captain allow me to pass
My mouth is as dry as the sands on the grass,
The Yankees are coming they are almost in sight
No beds will you find in Atlanta tonight.

Then I pray you young soldier my orders forgo
But fly not to the valley of the sweet Shenandoah,
Our bridges are down, our rivers are crossed
From Richmond to Shiloe our armies are lost.

With sabre and shell our soldiers are dying
Our daughters have fled and our widows are crying,
With none to oppose them they sweep to the sea
Oh gold help us young soldier and Robert E Lee.

Oh my captain, my captain, then let us away,
To the temples of glory that awaits us this day,
For long ere that sun has lost its sweet light
A bed in Atlanta we shall rest in tonight.

THE WREATH

Oh pretty flowers of Quiberon
With petals blue and gold
How many garlands have you made
How many have you sold?

Snow white roses for my bride
Which so much pleasure gave,
That even now their petals weep
Around the altars of her grave.

So make me a wreath of pretty flowers
With a poppy here and there,
To match the sunlight in her eyes
And the ribbon in her hair.

Tie it tight with pretty string
And a sash of ruby red
For much of love lies bound therein
Among those poppies upon her bed.

Oh pretty flowers of Quiberon
That lie on purple fields
Which throughout the years now left to me
No further pleasure yields.

FLORENCE AND MARY

What heaven may ordain
I do not know,
Nor would I ask of heaven and more
Than that those most dearly loved
Shall ere be blessed
With a candle in the window
And a lantern above their door
As dearly loved as they are to me
For never forms of human shape,
Angelic wings I could not see
Impressed so much the heart's desire
As dearly loved as you are to me.
So carefully now I tread the soil
The carpeted snow for fear a roar,
May blow away a dream of love
The cheerful reign of two angels
So close to me next door.